THE BOOK OF RIMBAUD

a e
i o u a e
i o u a e i
e i o u a e i
i e o u a e i
i o i

KEITH ABBOTT

THE BOOK OF

RIMBAUD

New Rivers Press 1977

other books by keith abbott:
    PUTTY (poems)
    WHAT YOU KNOW WITH NO NAME FOR IT (poems)
    12 SHOT (poems)
    GUSH (a novel)

parts of this book appeared in STRANGE FAECES

this book has been published with the aid of grants from the
New York State Council on the Arts and the National
Endowment for the Arts

this book was manufactured in the United States of America
at the Print Center in Brooklyn, N. Y. for New Rivers Press
(c. w. truesdale, editor/publisher), P. O. Box 578, Cathedral
Station, New York, N. Y. 10025 in a first edition of 750
copies of which 15 have been signed and numbered by the
author

PERSONAL NOTE ON THE BOOK OF RIMBAUD

In early 1972 I became interested in certain psychic phenomena. Toward the end of the year I happened to pick up a book on a murder case in Detroit where a psychic was involved (somewhat unsuccessfully). I read some more books on psychic phenomena and started to pay more attention to certain manifestations in my life. The connection between what I termed *imagination* and what others called psychic phenomena became clearer.

Coinciding with this interest was a series of prose poems where my mind seemed to slip out of the usual tracking patterns and become exposed to various visual / verbal / audial experiences. The poems were often strange, often without an objective rationale for their being. Some were static pictures and some were just voices. Many involved actions with characters of various sorts doing things.

During a time I was studying Artaud, I put myself in one of these states and instead of a poem, I had a tremendously vivid experience of seeing Artaud seated on a couch, looking around, appearing vaguely disatisfied. At the same time I was watching him, I worried because I was afraid he might speak and my French not be sufficient to understand him.

I became more curious about the nature of the will in some of my prose poems after that. Previously, what I would call my will seemed to destroy or damage the fabric of a poem (or trace state), and yet with the new prose poems I was writing, my will was present. Years ago I had trained myself for a while to wake up and write down dreams, or, change the dreams while dreaming, and it was similar to this. Anyway the presence of what I would call my will was not damaging to the experience, just as the presence of my worry over Artaud speaking had not damaged the experience, yet it was a manifestation of my will *inside the experience.*

In the spring of 1973 I was trying to reread Rimbaud with little luck. The poems were beyond my reading ability because they had been too long in my mind and were warped beyond help. I literally couldn't read them when I tried. One day in May I conceived of taking images from Rimbaud which I had memorized and sending them into the trance state, since as I explained my will was present and I could do that easily. The lines acted like tracers, illuminating rather odd landscapes and even odder actions. Sometimes the scenes I witnessed were slightly altered re-runs of the poems from which the lines came, and sometimes they were completely different from the context of the tracer lines. The exercise gave birth to *The Book of Rimbaud*.

I would like to thank Pat Nolan and Charles Wright for reading the much larger and much more chaotic first draft of the poems and making suggestions and comments on the text.

The final arrangement of the pieces, however, is all mine.

THE BOOK OF RIMBAUD

1.

Even though Rimbaud was dressed in a coarse black suit with baggy brown pants, the white shirt open at the neck and the buttons as pale as a calf's eye, I never saw him that way.

His face was a blur and the hair, dark brown, seemed stiff and the way it was situated on his head seemed to be almost an afterthought, *a thatch of brown hair only.*

When he turned, the cigarette up to his lips, I saw him as a burnt mask with the level brown plains behind his head dotted with low bushes.

When he wasn't there, somehow the fuchsias seemed to be him, hanging there with their waxy purple and red and white petals, their peeling paper bark. . . .

And underneath, the stones sparkling with dew, shaped in numbers and embedded in the earth like the dismembered addresses of the dead.

2.

Inside the carriage window panes I could see the dead moving around. Their mouths were worrying on words as if they couldn't say them. Rimbaud noticed me watching them. He leaned over and pointed at one old man in white, a night shirt, who was twisting his head this way and that like a raw necked bird begging for food.

"This is the manufacturer's wish. The dead prevent the glass from shattering should we get in a wreck, just as they prevent your mind from shattering when someone dies. The dead are here on earth to protect the living from the shock of dying."

Suddenly Rimbaud grinned at me as he pretended to say this and I was almost believing him when his teeth began to flow into a rainbow between his lips.

3.

"To achieve an absolute sense of innocence, or what is left of it," Rimbaud was saying as he adjusted the microphone on the long grey table. I had the feeling that we were at some sort of conference or interview but the chairs in front were as yet unfilled, some of them were already in an advanced state of decay, oozing a kind of grey cheese-like substance as they melted back into the floor from where they'd risen.

The microphone was a small conical object mounted on a stainless steel rod. Reflected in the steel was a group of men seated around the table, even though no one was in the room. The microphone was wet with sweat as bees clambered around it with their slow insect patience. . . .

4.

Rimbaud's cane was made of smoke. He waved it in the air and it would disappear. Then, when his hand stopped, it would reform and he would stick one end in his mouth and breathe deeply, his eyes mocking me.

5.

"Edges and edges, you see them slicing through me, like
this," Rimbaud turned slowly around, the sections of himself
falling in dark thin ribbons, black coat and white shirt sliced
to ribbons, curling down in the soft afternoon breeze.

6.

Under the rock's shadow the earthen jar had a series of incisions on it. The band was about four inches wide and the tool had been a blade of some sort, the slash deep and sharpedged, the shadows filling them like dark rain as the light from the setting sun glazed the top of the rock.

7.

The cave was damp and dark, wet streams trickled down the
walls. The light along one chipped hump in the wall seemed
bluish and white, as if light were being changed to rock, right
there.

8.

"One of my follies," Rimbaud said. We were watching the
line of men at the back of the cave with black rubber bulbs
for heads. They were sticking their brass stomachs into the
electrical outlets that dotted the wall. When their bellies
fitted the outlet's indention, they wriggled and squirmed as if
in some sort of ecstasy until they dropped exhausted to the
damp floor.

9.

The opera company seemed very poor. In fact they were almost dressed in rags as they meandered about on the wet ledge at the back of the cave. One lady was dressed as a maid-in-waiting, with a conical hat on top of her head but the scarf was tattered and a dirty blue.

A dwarf was turning handstands in front of an old man seated behind a badly stained red desk. The old man had white whiskers which grew out of his cheeks like strands of nylon fishing line. He was yelling about the court being brought to order while banging a gavel on the desk.

Rimbaud shouted over the echoes reverberating around the cave and the banging was so loud I had to close my eyes and put my hands over my ears. When I looked up, the judge had turned into a huge black sledgehammer, pounding and pounding on the floor of the cave.

10.

Out the cave window the snowy top of the mountain range seemed to give a chill to the classically pure notes the rabbit was playing, his right foot thumping softly on the keyboard, the piano gushing out streams of water that went meandering across the parquetry floor, which was polished immaculately except where the little bunches of violets sprouted from sooty cracks.

11.

To the left of the cave wall was a half finished figure of a heavy woman, her back being already carved in the white limestone, the huge bustle almost a distortion, the face and front still rough and porous.

Down her back were three streams of water, the one in the middle much larger than the two on the sides.

The stone was shaped so the dress seemed to be trying to pull itself free from the damp floor of the cave.

12.

Inside a long corridor I could see the lean white figure of
Rimbaud's mother. For a moment I thought she was a scare-
crow but the walls and floor were so dull, not even a glimmer
of light along the molding, it was all flat grey, I couldn't
imagine the least bit of greenery there. She had her mouth
open and periodically I heard a steam whistle, very loud and
very full.

13.

"The miracle of the waking world," he said, "is like the neck of a bottle. Underneath it everything is red and wet and drunken." He held up a cream-colored bone letter opener, as if to illustrate his point. Seeing my confusion, he laughed and laughed.

14.

The stairway went up to a needle's point somewhere below
the shadowy round ceiling. Rimbaud urged me up and al-
though I was apprehensive, I began walking step by step and
soon I was unaware of any stairs under my feet but seemed
to be inspecting a red tile roof, noting the little tufts of moss
with the spore pods nodding up out of the green fuzz like
delicate black antennae.

15.

Above the glitter of the silver plate Rimbaud lifted a calla lily and proposed a toast. We all stood and I noticed for the first time that the rest of the dinner guests were all animals, mostly beasts of burden, asses, oxen, and horses, except for the slim black lady at the head of the table who was completely naked under an outsized suit of polished armor.

16.

THE TABLEAU

The bed spilled over in furs. She spoke soft and low, in accents that matched her angular face, of the way evenings gathered in her home town.

The gleam off the half empty wine bottle turned one patch of sunlight on the floor green.

17.

HIS SONG FROM THE DEAD

The shadows of the branches on the windows, the shadows of
the windows on the floor,

The minaret of the bedpost shadow on the faded red rug, the
cool white window sill rubbed on a cheek,

The long black stairs, narrow and dangerous, and the first
sunlight on the rough red woolen coat sleeve.

18.

The soft green mounds of trees waving under the beige rim of
the stadium and on the green stretching out from the trees
the tents, all of them empty, the wind flapping the bright
tri-colored canvas.

Between the tents white fuzzy bundles blocked our way and
we stepped over them as we strolled along the exhibits. I
thought for a moment that the bundles were cocoons, for I
believed that I could see something black stirring inside
them.

Rimbaud was pointing out the empty tents as if they each
contained something and each time his lips would move to
say what was there, the words seemed to be blown by the
wind back over his cheeks and around his head.

19.

As we turned the corner of the rose garden, a rough patch of canvas appeared to be growing out of the lawn, as if it were the floor of a tent whose sides had flown off. Streaks of green disfigured the pure white expanse of canvas, and a smear of black as if someone's freshly polished boot had been dragged across it seemed somehow sad to me, as if an abduction had taken place.

20.

The two children were trapped inside some large garden tea rose bushes, the red petals blooming around them in slow motion, and they played on, a girl and a boy, peacefully unaware that they were floating inside a hedge of red rose bushes, the branches a waxy green and the thorns dark and sharp.

21.

Rimbaud lifted the curtain of green grass and showed me the feet, brown and muddy, that were marching underneath. The boots were ripped and tattered, leather scraps wound carefully around the tops to hold them close to the legs, and just as I was about to reach out and touch them, I found my hand resting on a small square of green turf.

22.

Despite the fact that the roof was rather steep, the lawn was growing on both sides of it. We climbed over the side of the giant tea cup that was holding the house and clambered up into the open doorway.

Inside the young lady in white was seated in a chair, right on the edge, her feet spread out, resting on her heels.

She partially undressed, leaving her white slip on, and then, she calmly bent over the unbuttoned Rimbaud's fly, taking his snub-nosed cock in her mouth as I eased up behind and raised her slip.

Just as I felt the warmth of her cleft on the head of my cock, I glanced behind me and saw the staircase to the second floor was nothing more than a stiff blue carpet leaning against the white balcony.

23.

In the peaceful green of the castle the cannon would have stood. Instead a graceful girl of 13, dressed in a white smock, did a little dance step around the gun carriage, apparently waiting for someone to come.

24.

Like some sort of top, the demon whirled in the red dust.
Rimbaud bent over and watched him. "Dervish," he said. He
almost mumbled it again but I only heard the "D" sound
come out.

Rimbaud turned and looked out at the huge ugly pillar of
salt that was sticking up out of the plain. All around us was
a green rolling lawn but it disappeared the moment either of
us would look directly at it.

25.

Off the path was a puddle of blood, dried black and reflect-
ing all the light back on us. Rimbaud leaned over and in-
spected it. "A mirror," he said softly.

26.

Just inside his back there was a discernable hump where the
demon lived. "He is no longer there," he remarked one day
when I was staring at the radio in the corner. I knew what
he meant. At the beach I had noticed his sandy spine as he
leaned over and regarded the sea with a tender air, "I'd
love to be a log, adrift, rolling over and over in the surf, worn
smooth...." There was no sign of a scar, just the bumps of
his spine, sandy and drying.

27.

"The name 'CHOCOLATE' was the one I gave whenever I would find myself face down on the bed, my head literally pounding." He says this with an expression of bitterness in his face, as if he has just eaten a handful of salt.

28.

"The cables came down from my brain," he explained, "and the curve of them in the sky was like the moon, thin and silvery, that stretch from the tip of my nose up into the front of my brain."

29.

Above the small dome of the sacredest marble was a thin triangular steeple, architecturally impossible so it was completely imaginary. Around the side of the church was a circular walkway, the weathered grey tombstones so stained with rain as to be almost green fanned out along the path.

In the dull red and grey gravel my feet almost felt a sense of triumph, as if I were walking along the most holy path in creation. I was dressed in satin, violet and maroon satin with an orange silk belt.

Even though I kept my eyes on the silver steeple above the dome, the soft rub of satin twined itself around my body.

"Have you noticed how we keep being children?" Rimbaud whispered during the quiet time in the services.

30.

"The mother is over here," he explained, using that patient tone I had come to dislike so much. He opened the wooden slat gate, the long rusty hinges stretched out along the boards like blunt fingers . . . inside the overhang of the rock was a woman, she was nursing some white rags, holding them up to her swollen brown nipples and rocking back and forth.

Rimbaud moved over to her and stared at her intently. Then, with one flick of his black boot, he kicked dust on her.

She raised her eyes to him, her eyes were dark brown and large, and abruptly she turned into a dead cactus stump, the sliced top shriveled and warped around the edges, the center sunken and brown as the water evaporated out of the opening.